Cocktails

Cookbook

60 of the World's Best Cocktail Drink Recipes from the Caribbean

& How to Mix Them at Home.

By

Grace Barrington-Shaw

More books by Grace Barrington-Shaw:

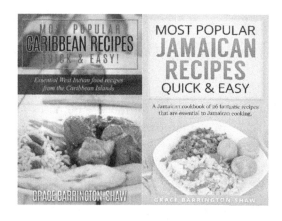

Disclaimer

All reasonable efforts have been made to provide accurate and error-free recipes within this book. These recipes are intended for use by persons possessing the appropriate technical skill, at their own discretion and risk. The author is not responsible or liable for any allergies, reactions, accidents or incidents of any kind that may arise as a result of cooking these recipes. It is advisable that you take full note of the ingredients before mixing and use substitutes where necessary, to fit your dietary requirements.

Contents

Introduction 7

FREE Bonuses 9

What is a Cocktail? 10

About Caribbean Cocktails 11

Ingredients 13

    Rums and Spirits 13

    Liqueurs 15

    Herbs, Spices and Garnishes 15

  Types of Exotic Drinks 16

Rum and Spirit Recipes 17

    Mojito 17

    Planter's Punch 19

    Blanchisseuse Rum Punch 21

    The Painkiller Cocktail 22

    Pina Colada 23

    Ti Punch 24

    Bahama Mama 25

    The Goombay Smash 27

    The Daiquiri 29

    Frozen Strawberry Daiquiri 30

    The Cuba Libre 31

    The Dark and Stormy 32

    Mai Tai Cocktail 33

    Elvis Rum Punch 34

    Pumphouse Rum Punch 35

    Frozen Rum Runners 36

Tropical Depression 37

Old Jamaican 38

Antiguan Smile 39

Santo Libre 40

Rum and coconut water 41

Sherwin Noel's Rum Punch 42

Tequila Recipes 43

About the Tequila: 43

The Ever Classic Tequila Sunrise 44

Hummingbird with a twist 45

The Margarita! 46

Long Island Iced Tea 48

Salty Chihuahua (with Lemonade) 49

Horny Bull 50

Mango margarita 51

Liqueur Recipes 52

Milano-Torino 52

Cold Shower 53

Purple Devil recipe 53

Safari Juice recipe 54

Tinyee's Orange Smoothie recipe 55

Mocha Maria recipe 56

Brown Cow recipe 57

Independence on Ice – with or without the rum 58

Frozen Toasted Almond 59

Non-Alcoholic Recipes (Mocktails) 60

Caribbean Sunset 60

Virgin Chi Chi 62

Pina Colada Mocktail 63

Fruit Loops 64

Afterglow 65

Ugly Virgin 66

Special Occasions 67

Weddings 67

Beach wedding 67

Spring and Summer weddings 69

Fall and Winter wedding 70

Other special occasions 70

Recommended Cocktails for Weddings 71

The Cayman Lemonade 71

Kapalua Sunrise 72

Caribbean Cruise 72

Vodka Passion Fruit Punch 73

Vodka Lola 74

Sparkling Sea Breeze 75

Honeydew Mimosa 75

White Cosmo 77

Tropical Champagne Punch 78

Tropical Itch 79

Aruba Ariba 80

Creating Your Own Cocktails 81

Cocktails Tools & Utensils 82

Measurements & Conversions 84

Thankyou 90

Introduction

On a cruise or a night out on the town, cocktails are your best bet for a great time. No matter the occasion, without a cocktail you are definitely missing out. In this book, we will introduce to you some of the best Caribbean cocktails, how they are made, their origin, and about their ingredients.

You will find cocktails for every palate and occasion; both alcoholic and non-alcoholic. The cocktails presented are done with a twist to help make them your own. We've substituted some of the rare ingredients with easy to find items that you can pick up in your local grocery store.

Cocktails provide a refreshing alternative to wines and liquors. While bourbons, whiskeys and brandies can be served on the rocks or neat, and are great for warming the stomach in cold climates, Caribbean cocktails are for keeping you cool. Most cocktails include the blending of ice cubes along with the main ingredients to offer an icy cold drink in warm weather.

You will find that all of, or most Caribbean resorts are known for their cocktails. Some even have their own special blends that are synonymous with their particular hotel brand.

Beaches are also known for their cocktails. Popular beach cocktail may be served in a coconut or a hollowed pineapple. Some many choose to serve their cocktail in a watermelon! Caribbean resorts will present their cocktails in weird and wonderful ways but the ingredients remain fundamental to the taste.

The younger members of the family can also enjoy a refreshing cocktail without the alcohol. Some drinks famous for their alcohol-free versions are the Daiquiri, Pina Colada and the Afterglow.

There is such a wide variety of cocktails but you do not have to be a trained bartender to mix your own, in this book we will show you how.

We have 3 **FREE** bonus cookbooks for your enjoyment!

- **Cookie Cookbook** 2134 recipes
- **Cake Cookbook** 2444 recipes
- **Mac and Cheese Cookbook** 103 recipes

Simply visit: www.ffdrecipes.com to get your **FREE recipe ebooks.**

You will also receive free exclusive access to our World Recipes Club, giving you FREE best-selling book offers, discounts and recipe ideas, delivered to your inbox regularly.

www.ffdrecipes.com

What is a Cocktail?

A cocktail is usually referred to as an alcoholic drink that's made up of some sort of rum/spirit and juice or rum and cream along with other ingredients. Some people may define it as a drink with three or more ingredients with one of those ingredients being alcohol.

In recent times, we've discovered that, not everyone can consume alcohol and so there are cocktails that do not contain the potent stuff. It is safe to say that a cocktail is a beverage with three ingredients or more that is enjoyed socially and recreationally.

The origin of the word cocktail has been disputed, but what we do know is that the first recorded use of the word was in the United States and may have referred to a concoction made for medical use. The first time it was used was definitely for a non-alcoholic drink and was recorded in the newspaper, The Farmer's Cabinet on April 28, 1803. The first recorded use which referenced alcohol was slightly later on in The Balance and Columbian Repository.

When asked what a cocktail was, the editor of that newspaper replied:

"Cocktail is a stimulating liquor, composed of spirits of any kind, sugar, water, and bitters—it is vulgarly called Bittered Sling, and is supposed to be an excellent electioneering potion, in as much as it renders the heart stout and bold, at the same time that it fuddles the head. It is said, also to be of great use to a democratic candidate: because a person, having swallowed a glass of it, is ready to swallow anything else"

About Caribbean Cocktails

Caribbean cocktails are famous the world over and are served in every hotel, resort, cruise lines, most pubs/bar and clubs, nightspots and party venues. Many special events will have a round of cocktails specially created for the event. These include weddings, anniversaries, birthdays, launch parties and conferences.

There is a cocktail for every occasion and age group. You will find the classics are suited for the older folks while the new generation will opt for new mixes with psychedelic colors.

Caribbean cocktails are famous for one thing, their main ingredient, the rum. We all know that the Caribbean is known for the most potent liquor around the world and perhaps the most drunken sailors... oh, well... not really. However, Caribbean rums are not the typical serve over ice drinks. They are made so potently that most of them must be used with what we call a chaser.

Take for instance the White Overproof Rum from Jamaica. Just try drinking this over ice and you are likely to experience a sensation similar to fire in your throat! With this in mind, please don't try this at home!

Many Caribbean cocktails were invented by accident, like the Pina Colada, one of the most well-known drinks ever to come out of the Caribbean. It was the handiwork of a coconut plantation owner while he had a party at a resort. Not knowing what to serve his guests, he decided to try his hand at something. Taking pressed pineapple juice, coconut cream, rum, and crushed ice, he made a drink that not only tasted great, but had his guests clamoring for more. That's what a Pina Colada will do, have you wanting more.

Many Caribbean cocktails were actually invented by non-Caribbean people, like the English bar owner Miss Emily for her version of the Bahama Mama. Though the version that became famous was actually created by someone else after she shared her secret.

The Caribbean cocktails' main requirement is that you use Caribbean ingredients or, at least, a rum or liqueur from the Caribbean.

Ingredients

Rums and Spirits

In case you are not familiar with what a rum, or spirit is here is a definition. Rum is a type of alcohol that is made using the distilling process. This type of alcohol derives from cane sugar or molasses and is one of the most potent alcohols in the world.

Some rums are single distilled while others are double distilled. There are different kinds of rums, but the three basic categories are white (or light), dark and red runs. Any of these rums can be double distilled for more of a mellow flavor, or overproof for a stronger taste.

Most rums have an alcoholic content by volume of 35% and goes up to 80 or 90%.

Proof is used to measure the alcohol content in rums. When the rum is being distilled there is a ratio of alcohol to water content. The proof is the measure of this ratio. No rum has alcohol that is higher than 95 to 5 percent alcohol to water. Alcohol produced at one hundred percent is used for scientific and medical purposes only.

The rum and spirit cocktails are the most popular drinks in the Caribbean. Rum is used every day and is the most sold alcohol in the tropic. It's used with a chaser, such as 'rum and coke', or with plain water as a solid rum drink. Some rums, depending on how they are produced, are mild while some are very intense. The milder, smoother rums can be had on the rocks while the more intense rums, such as the Jamaican Overproof White Rum, must be had in a cocktail or with a chaser. This rum is too 'hot' to be had on the rocks or neat.

Other rums include the best of Caribbean

Zacapa rum (Guatemala)

Appleton Estate and Appleton Estate Special (Jamaica)

Tortuga (Cayman Islands)

Myers Dark Rum (Jamaica)

Pussers Rum (British Virgin Islands)

Blackwell (Jamaica)

White Overproof (Jamaica)

Malibu (Barbados) is a flavored rum

White Coconut Rum (Jamaica)

Don Q (Puerto Rico)

Mount Gay (Barbados)

Cruzan Rums (St, Croix) is a suite of light, dark and flavored rums.

Bacardi (Puerto Rico)

El Dorado (Guyana)

Havana Club (Cuba) a suite of light and dark rums

Liqueurs

A liqueur is a type of alcohol that is made from distilled alcoholic beverages. These liqueurs are flavored with fruit, cream, herbs, spices, flowers or nuts and has been sweetened to enhance the flavor. Sweeteners may include sugar, syrups, fruit juices and honey or molasses.

Popular liqueurs include:

Tia Maria coffee liqueur – a liqueur made from coffee, rum, sugar and vanilla. It makes wonderful cocktails with coffee lovers in mind. It can be had over ice for a real ice-coffee drink with a kick.

Pimento (Allspice) liqueur – made from the ripened berries of the allspice, otherwise known as pimentos, vanilla and sugar.

Triple Sec - Originated from Curacao and is a triple distilled liqueur made from the dried peel of oranges. It is one of the widest used cocktail flavorings in the Caribbean and many mixologists are never without it. It has been used in hundreds of cocktails and is very delicious on its own. Use at home to spice up your summer drink or when you have company over.

Herbs, Spices and Garnishes

Every cocktail needs a special flavor or garnish. The most common herb used in making cocktails is the spearmint, or as Jamaican's call it, the black mint. The leaf of this mint is tender and bruises easily. The flavor is not too potent, yet strong enough to add zest to any food or drink. This is the mint used in cooking the world over and is used in numerous amounts of cocktails.

Blended – using a blender to make these cocktails usually involves ice and fruits that need crushing or pureeing.

Stirred – Stirred drinks often involve light juices and mixes that combine easily.

Shaken – The cocktail shaker is used to mix drinks with special flavors. In some cases you will have crushed lemon or mint leaves and then added your liquids. In other cases you add a few cubes of ice and then pour off your drink, leaving the mint or ice behind.

Fruity – fruit drinks are lighter and more refreshing. These are consumed mostly by those who cannot consume alcohol and by children. A popular fruity cocktail is the Daiquiri.

Mojito

The Mojito is Cuba's signature drink and is probably the most widely known Caribbean cocktail. It is known worldwide by both locals and foreigners. This drink is surprisingly easy to make and has a very refreshing taste.

The Mojito dates back from the sixteenth century. We believe this drink was invented by Francis Drake's crew, when they crushed mint leaves, added lime and rum to create a unique blend. Since then, the drink has become famous and no one goes to Cuba without trying it once!

Even famous people like Hemmingway have had the Mojito. It was also the signature drink of the James Bond movie, Die Another Day, with Peirce Brosnan and Halle Berry.

Ingredients

2 sprigs of mint, plus one for garnish

1 teaspoon superfine sugar

2 ounces light rum

1/2 cup cracked ice

Club soda

Lime wedge

Preparation

In a cocktail shaker, muddle mint with superfine sugar. Pour in rum and add cracked ice. Shake well. Strain the contents into a tall glass with ice, and then top it off with chilled club soda. Garnish the beverage with a wedge of lime and a sprig of mint and enjoy.

Note: Make this as potent or as light as you need. For a stronger drink, add more rum. You can also have a virgin mojito by omitting the rum altogether.

Popular planter's punch saying: "A wine-glass with lemon juice fill, of sugar the same glass fill twice/Then rub them together until/The mixture looks smooth, soft, and nice. Of rum then three wine glasses add, /And four of cold water please take. A drink then you'll have that's not bad / At least, so they say in Jamaica."

One of the most potent cocktails found anywhere, The Planters Punch has around 44.7 percent alcohol content. This drink is an official cocktail of the International Bartenders' Association. It includes dark rum, lemon juice, grenadine syrup and Angostura bitters. This drink is also said to include herbs and spices originating from Trinidad and Tobago. So, even though it was originated in Jamaica, it is more accurate to classify it as purely... Caribbean.

Here is the secret to the planter's punch. One part lemon, two parts sugar, three parts rum and four parts juice.

Ingredients

1 ounce fresh lemon juice

2 tablespoons sugar

3 ounces light rum

4 ounces orange juice

Ice

Preparation

Place all ingredients in a cocktail shaker.

Shake well.

Strain into a chilled glass and garnish with a lemon wedge, if desired.

Variations

Here is the trick, you may substitute your orange juice with another juice or, add one ounce juice from four fruits for a unique flavor. Also add one ounce dark and two ounces light rum, for a kick.

Blanchisseuse Rum Punch

Named after the beach called Blanchisseuse, located in a small village in the northern cost of Trinidad, this cocktail is believed to be a little more complicated to concoct than most. It involves tangerine and Portugal juice.

Ingredients

1 oz - freshly squeezed Caribbean lime juice

2 tsp superfine cane sugar or 2 oz cane juice

3 oz - dark Trinidad rum

4 oz - freshly squeezed tangerine otherwise known as Portugal.

Preparation

Add all ingredients to a cocktail shaker and shake well. Add ice cube to glass and pour in your drink with a few drops of angostura bitters. Garnish with lime or oranges slices. You may also add sugar to the rim of your glass for extra garnish.

Another variation is to add nutmeg instead of the bitters:

The tangerine (Portugal fruit) juice is the secret ingredient in this concoction and is said to give it an exotic flavor. There is also another fruit known as the mandarin that has a similar flavor and can be used as substitute. I suppose if you are out of either fruits the orange can be used, but I warn you, oranges are much tarter than the Portugal and the taste is distinctly different.

The Painkiller Cocktail

I often consider what was being thought of when they named this drink. Perhaps the insanely huge amount of alcohol will numb your pain? This drink was created by none other than an English lady herself, Daphne Henderson of the Soggy Dollar Bar on Jost Van Dyke island.

However, the drink was only made famous after she shared her secrets with Charles Tobias who then owned Pusser's distillery and made his own version using his own rum! Wow, talk about stealing the show. After a taste test was done, it was determined that Charles Tobias' version was better.

Ingredients

2-4 oz. of Pusser's Rum

4 oz. pineapple juice

1 oz. cream of coconut

1 oz. orange juice

Grated fresh nutmeg

Pina Colada

Probably the most famous of all the cocktails and definitely the most widely served not only in the Caribbean but the rest of the world. This drink is so famous that there is Pina Colada mix that anyone can purchase from their local store. All you need to do is add ice and maybe another splash of rum if you so please.

This drink was accidentally created, or rather created out of a dire need, by Ricardo Garcia, who was a coconut plantation owner, and a Caribbean resident originating from Barcelona. In 1914, the coconut workers on his plantation went on a strike. He was stretched for ingredients to make cocktails for his guests and decided to try his hand at mixing the pineapple juice with coconut cream and rum and poured the concoctions into hollowed pineapples. This proved to be a hit and now, his invention is probably the most famous cocktail invention ever.

Ingredients

3 oz (3 parts) Pineapple juice

1 oz (one part) White rum

1 oz (one part) Coconut cream

This is one of the simplest drinks to make, but do not underestimate the taste. On any given occasion cane juice is very refreshing, add a splash of lime and some rum and you've got a killer cocktail. This cocktail is very popular in Martinique and Guadeloupe.

The good thing about the Ti Punch is that you can make it whenever you please. Add as much rum and lime to your taste. Usually patrons are given the bottle of rum, a pitcher of cane juice and some limes to fix their own drink. Have it your way!

Ingredients

Cane juice

Lime

Rum

Preparation

Combine all three ingredients and serve in highball glass over ice. Garnish with lime wedge or slice.

Bahama Mama

This drink is made using quite a number of ingredients and many people shy away from it. It's not usually a drink that you would want to make for a simple party, but if you do then you won't regret it. This cocktail was first made in the Bahamas during the Prohibition era when the island was known to be famous for smuggling. The Bahama Mama is usually served in a hollowed coconut.

Ingredients (The original recipe)

¼ oz coffee liqueur

½ oz dark rum

½ oz coconut liqueur

¼ oz 151 proof rum

½ of a lemon - juiced

4 oz pineapple juice

Preparation

Combine all ingredients and pour over cracked ice in a Collins glass. Decorate with a strawberry or cherry and serve.

Ingredients (Variations)

½ oz lemon juice

2 oz orange juice

2 oz pineapple juice

1 ½ oz rum

1 oz coconut rum

½ oz cherry liqueur

½ oz grenadine syrup

Preparation

Shake ingredients with cracked ice. Serve in a 12 oz. glass. Garnish with a cherry and 1/2 slice orange in a tooth pick.

The Goombay Smash

The Blue Bee Bar on Great Turtle Cay, located in the Bahamas is to be credited for this wonderful cocktail. Hold your seats, because this potent drink contains four different rums. Can you believe that this very special cocktail was created by a woman, Miss Emily? Yes indeed. It seems the most concentrated of these cocktails were created by the female specie! This drink is now the national drink of the Bahamas!

There is something you need to know before making this drink. You cannot call it a Goombay Smash if all four rums aren't included, however, you can adjust the quantity of each rum to your taste. This recipe serves two.

Ingredients

Ice cubes

6 tablespoons pineapple juice

¼ cup orange juice

¼ cup coconut-flavored rum

2 tablespoons light rum

2 tablespoons gold rum

2 tablespoons dark rum

2 pineapple wedges

2 orange slices

Preparation

Fill cocktail shaker with ice; add pineapple juice, orange juice, and all rum. Cover and shake until very cold. Fill 2 short glasses with ice. Strain cocktail mixture over, dividing equally. Garnish with pineapple wedges and orange slices. Don't get drunk too quickly or you won't be able to enjoy another.

This is another popular cocktail that can be made with or without the rum. It is believed that the Daiquiri was named after a beach close to or within Santiago. This drink perhaps has the most variety of any cocktail there is because of the various fruits that can be used.

It was around the 1950s that this drink became an international sensation when it was served to tourists in Havana. The fist versions were flavored with maraschino cherry liqueur and the original is still available today at the Old Havana.

There are different variations to this drink. There are the blended fruity versions, mostly non-alcoholic and the simple version. Here are two alcoholic versions. Please see non-alcoholic section for other variations.

Simplest version. Substitute Lime juice with any other citrus.

Ingredients

1 ½ oz White rum,

½ oz Simple syrup,

1 oz Lime juice

Preparation

Pour all ingredients into shaker with ice cubes. Shake well. Strain in chilled cocktail glass.

Garnish with lime slice.

Frozen Strawberry Daiquiri
(substitute strawberry for any other frozen fruit)

Ingredients

6 cups ice

½ cup white sugar

4 ounces frozen strawberries

1/8 cup lime juice

½ cup lemon juice

¾ cup rum

¼ cup Sprite (or other lemon-lime flavored carbonated drink)

Preparation

In a blender, combine ice, sugar and strawberries. Pour in lime juice, lemon juice, rum and lemon-lime soda. Blend until smooth. Pour into glasses and serve.

This is probably the simplest cocktail ever. It's really just a twist on the rum and coke. When I say twist, I mean a real twist, because all you need is a twist of lime and you've got yourself the Cuba Libre. The name is credited to the Spanish American war when the American troops were determined to liberate Cuba from the Spanish. If you go to a bar and order rum and coke, you are ordering a Cuba Libre.

Ingredients

4 oz Cola

1/3 oz Fresh lime juice

1 2/3 oz White rum

Preparation

Remember that coke is fizzy so you cannot shake, but you can use a swizzle stick to stir. So add all ingredients to a highball glass with ice and stir. Garnish with a lime wedge or slice.

Now, here is a twist to the Cuba Libre which some Jamaicans have invented. Instead of 4 oz coke, add 2 oz coke and 2 oz lager beer.

You can also use red rum for this recipe for a mellower rum flavor. The amount of rum you use is totally up to you, depending on how potent you like it.

Another simple drink that is a favorite of many people. However, beware, because without the dark Gosling rum and Barritt's ginger beer you may have mayhem on your hands. Many people will argue that, without the original ingredients you cannot rightly call it Dark and Stormy. We beg to differ.

Ingredients

3 1/3 oz Ginger Beer

Couple dashes of bitters

2 oz Dark Rum

Preparation

In a highball glass filled with ice, add dark rum and top with ginger beer. Garnish with lime wedge.

You can also add the ginger bear first over the ice then float the dark rum on tip. There is another drink called the ginger ale which can be used. Ginger ale is slightly different and has a crisper flavor.

The invention of this drink is still in debate as to who created it. The first noted version of the drink came about sometime in 1937 by a man called Don The Beachcomber. However, another version later surfaced in 1944 by Trader Vic, who claimed her had no prior knowledge of the drink. This provokes a question; how can two drinks be exactly the same? Well, we are still in the dark about who first came up with this drink, but what we do know, is that people just can't get enough of it.

Ingredients:

1 ½ oz White rum

½ oz Fresh lime juice

½ oz Orange curacao

½ oz Orgeat syrup

¾ oz Dark rum

Preparation

Shake all ingredients except the dark rum together in a mixer with ice. Strain into glass, then slowly pour the dark rum onto the top to float. Garnish with lime peel, lime wedges or pineapple spear. Serve with straw.

Elvis Rum Punch

I'm not sure if this cocktail has anything to do with "The Elvis", but I do know it's very irresistible. The ingredients alone speak for themselves.

Ingredients

1 oz. orange juice

1 oz. pineapple juice

1 oz. guava juice

1/2 oz. lime juice

3 dashes of bitters

3 oz. red or dark rum

Amaretto

Nutmeg

Preparation

In a shaker add first pineapple juice, guava juice, lime juice, bitters, rum and orange juice. Add ice and shake.

Pour in a highball glass. Add an Amaretto floater and sprinkle with nutmeg.

Pumphouse Rum Punch

Ingredients

1 part fresh lime juice

2 parts liquid cane syrup

3 parts red or dark rum

4 parts ice

A few dashes Angostura bitters

Preparation

Pour all ingredients in a shaker and mix well. Pour into glasses and top with a little freshly grated nutmeg.

Ingredients

1 ounce gold rum

1/4 ounce blackberry liqueur

1/4 ounce creme de banana liqueur

2 ounces orange juice

1/2 ounce grenadine

8 ounces crushed ice

1/2 oz. dark rum

Preparation

Add gold rum, blackberry liqueur, creme de banana liqueur, orange juice, grenadine and crushed ice in a blender. Blend until slushy and pour into glass. Float with the 1/2 oz. dark rum.

Ingredients

2 oz. mango purée

2 oz. strawberry purée

1 oz dark rum

1 oz triplesec

1 oz amaretto

1 oz coconut crème

Preparation

Blend all ingredients with ice until smooth. Pour into a short glass and garnish with toasted coconut, pineapple and maraschino cherries.

Old Jamaican

Ingredients

1 oz. lime juice

1 ½ oz. of rum

¾ oz simple syrup,

1 dash of Angostura bitters

1 sprig mint

Preparation

Muddle 1 sprig of mint in a shaker using a pestle. Add all ingredients except for champagne and shake well. Pour over ice and splash the top with champagne. Serve.

Ingredients

2 oz rum

1 oz crème de banana

4 oz fresh pineapple juice

Preparation

In a cocktail shaker place rum, crème de banana and pineapple juice and shake. Serve over ice and garnish with pineapple.

Ingredients

Rum of your choice

Lemon lime or club soda

Fresh lime

Preparation

Fill a tall glass with ice, add rum and splash on soda. Add a squeeze of fresh lime. Garnish with lime slice and serve.

Rum and coconut water

The classic Caribbean refreshing drink, not only reserved for parties but any time of day.

Ingredients

Rum (red or white)

Coconut water

Lime

Ice

Preparation

Streetside or on the beach: Ask for a chilled jelly coconut, add rum and a squeeze of lime. Place a straw in the coconut and enjoy.

Fill a tall glass with ice and add the rum. Pour in your coconut water and add a squeeze of lime. Garnish with lime slice or lime peel. Enjoy!

For a kick, add a dash of angostura bitters.

Ingredients

3 oz dark rum

3 oz overproof rum

½ oz sugar syrup

½ cup Grapefruit juice

½ Orange juice

½ Pineapple juice

Juice of 1 sour orange

Juice of 2 limes

Grenadine

Angostura bitters

Preparation

In a pitcher, combine juices and rum. Add grenadine and bitters. Serve over ice in highball glass. Sprinkle top with freshly grated nutmeg.

Tequila Recipes

About the Tequila:

The most famous tequila recipe, except for the lime and salt shots, is the margarita. As the name suggests, this is primarily a Mexican cocktail. The tequila is the most sought after Central American alcohol and is known throughout the world for shots.

Let me tell you something about Tequila that you may not know. Let's talk about the worm, yes, the Tequila worm! Many people complain that there isn't a worm in their tequila and refuse to have their drink until they understand why it isn't so.

However, why would there be a worm in the tequila and what purpose does it serve?

Now here is the deal. Tequila does NOT carry worms, or rather, they aren't supposed to. The worms are usually found in what is called mescal, a home brewed alcohol that the locals usually consume because the real thing was too expensive.

This worm is actually a butterfly larva that is found in a pineapple like plant used to make this mescal drink. Back to the question of why there is a worm in the tequila. Actually, the worm was deliberately placed in the Tequila bottle as a marketing strategy by no other than Jacobo Lozano Paez! Yes, he made a lot of money and a name for himself selling those worms.

So next time you visit an establishment, please don't get upset at the bartender about the lack of a worm in your tequila! A popular question is whether these worms have a certain effect on you? Perhaps, as they are thought to be aphrodisiacs which explains why they are so popular!

Now here are some very delicious tequila recipes to make your party sizzle.

The Ever Classic Tequila Sunrise

Ingredients

2 oz tequila

Fresh orange juice

1 tbsp grenadine

Crushed ice

Preparation

You can blend or shake this recipe, but the trick to get the sunrise is to leave out the grenadine and add it last. Here's what to do. To a blender, add ice, tequila, orange juice and blend. Pour in a glass and then pour in the grenadine which will sink to the bottom of the drink. Do not stir!

To shake it, add all the ingredients, except for the grenadine to the shaker, then pour over ice and add the grenadine last. Remember not to stir.

Here's another method: Add ice to glass, pour in tequila, then orange juice and the grenadine. Do not stir!

This is a different take on the classic tequila cocktail called the hummingbird in which tangerine sage leaves are used. Now we have changed the sage to mint leaves to give a different, more refreshing flavor. As you know mint has a cooling effect and these drinks are best had during warm weather to keep you cool.

Ingredients

4 mint leaves

¾ oz fresh lime juice

2tsp grenadine

2 oz tequila

Preparation

First, bruise the mint leaves in a cocktail shaker, add your tequila, lime juice and grenadine with ice. Shake vigorously and then pour into a chilled glass. Garnish with fresh mint leaf or lime peel.

The Margarita!

This cocktail is one of the best known around the world. If you've ever been anywhere in Central America, the tropics and some places in the US, you've most likely heard of this. Every adult pool party, beach party and any kind of party has this treat.

The ingredients in the cocktail are to die for. You can have this drink blended shaken or stirred, depending on your preference.

On a warm summer day at the beach, you'll want to have your margarita blended with ice. On a hot summer night, you will have this shaken and served over ice. In the cooler temperatures you'll have this stirred and taken without the ice.

Ingredients

2 oz Tequila

1 oz Lime juice

1 oz Triplesec

Preparation

Rub the rim of the glass with the lime slice to ensure the salt sticks to it. Shake the other ingredients with ice, then carefully pour into the glass (taking care not to dislodge any salt). Garnish and serve over ice.

Now, here's a popular twist to this recipe:

Tequila

Lemon juice (you can use limes, but you know lime are tarter than lemons)

Simple syrup (pure made from refined white sugar)

Triplesec

Ice

In a blender add ice, tequila lemon juice and syrup. Blend until slushy. Rub the rim of the glass with lime, then add salt or sugar (depending on your taste), pour into glass and garnish with lemon peel or lemon slice.

Another trick is to use different kinds of syrup to give different colors and flavors to your margarita!

Don't be fooled, this is not iced tea! This is not the kind of drink you sit and sip on a hot summer afternoon with your kids. This is the kind of drink you have with friends, or you significant other and only if there is a designated driver.

The reason why it was called an iced tea is because of the color after the coke is mixed in. In fact, it does bear a resemblance to iced tea.

Ingredients

1 part vodka

1 part tequila

1 part rum

1 part gin

1 part triple sec

1 1/2 parts sweet and sour mix

1 splash Coke (the beverage) or other cola

Preparation

Mix ingredients together over ice in a glass. Pour into a shaker and give one brisk shake. Pour back into the glass and make sure there is a touch of fizz at the top. Garnish with lemon.

Salty Chihuahua (with Lemonade)

This is one of the easiest, most refreshing tequila cocktails you will ever have. As long as you have tequila you have no problem. Other than the tequila of course, the other main ingredient is lemonade. Who doesn't have lemonade at home? If you are in the Caribbean or other warm climate, you are sure to have lemonade in your refrigerator to cool off from the heat.

Ingredients

1 ½ oz. tequila

5 oz. lemonade

Splash of lime juice

Lime wedge, and coarse salt or sugar for garnish (optional)

Preparation

Rub some lime on the rim of the glass, then sugar or salt the moist rim (the lime allows the sugar or salt to hold). Fill glass with ice. Pour in tequila and lemonade. Squeeze and drop in lime wedge for a splash of lime juice. Stir and serve.

Horny Bull

With, only two ingredients! This is must try for everyone, and if you are a cocktail drinker, you'll be sure to have a bottle of tequila in your possession. This is very simple to make at home so no further need to order at the bar.

Ingredients

2 oz. tequila

Orange juice

Preparation

Fill tall glass with ice and pour in tequila. Stir 2-3 times. Top off with orange juice and serve.

Now here is a little twist to this recipe that you may love. Add a little dash of crème de menthe for a lively taste!

Mango margarita

Ingredients

1 oz. tequila

1 oz. triple sec

2 oz. simple syrup

2 1/2 oz. mango purée

Juice from half a lemon

Preparation

In a blender combine all ingredients with ice and blend until smooth.

Garnish with lime or orange slice and serve. Ole!

Liqueur Recipes

Liqueur is the flavored, less potent alcoholic beverage that is usually used alongside the more potent stuff to flavor your cocktail. It does have a certain amount of alcohol, but in far lesser volume. It is usually very sweet and used as flavoring only. It can be used alongside juices and chasers to create a milder alcoholic cocktail. For the person who is just starting to experience alcohol, young adults, and the elderly, using liqueur to make your cocktail is the preferred route to take. Enjoy these low alcohol cocktails made from various liqueurs from around the Caribbean.

Milano-Torino

The primary liqueur in this drink is Campari, a bitter sweet liqueur used to give cocktails a unique flavor. Campari can be had over ice or made into sumptuous drinks that you will keep craving.

Ingredients

1 part Sweet Vermouth

1 part Campari

Preparation

Using a tulip glass, fill halfway with ice. Pour in the Campari and then the sweet Vermouth

To add zest to this drink, squeeze a little orange juice in it straight from a peeled orange. Add an orange slice to garnish and you're good to go.

Cold Shower

Ingredients

Since this drink is so refreshing it could not be given a more suitable name!

1 part green creme de menthe

4 parts club soda

Preparation

Using a highball glass add ice, your creme de menthe and then the club soda. Stir and enjoy.

Purple Devil recipe

Ingredients

1 part triple sec

1 part orange liqueur

1 part almond liqueur

Cranberry juice

1 splash lemon-lime soda

Preparation

Combine liqueur with ice in shaker. Using a highball glass fill with ice and strain the chilled liqueur combo. Add Cranberry to ¾ way up and top off with the lemon-lime soda. Garnish with lime or orange slice or peel.

Ingredients

30 ml orange liqueur

30 ml melon liqueur

140 ml orange juice

6 drops grenadine syrup

Preparation

This recipe is done best when mixed and not shaken. Combine orange and melon liqueur in a mixing glass and stir. Add orange juice and stir vigorously four times. In a chilled highball or cocktail glass, add ice, then pour in your drink. Add the grenadine drops one at a time (do not stir), garnish with melon or orange.

Tinyee's Orange Smoothie recipe

This drink is guaranteed to put the tropics into the Caribbean. The orange is essentially the essence of this recipe but what if you don't like orange? What if you prefer other types of tropical fruit? Why not change around the fruits, fruit juices and perhaps the liqueur to suit your taste? The secret with this drink is that the liqueur must match the main fruit, so if you would like a melon smoothie, simply use melon juice and melon liqueur. Likewise, for an apple smoothie you would use apple juice and apple liqueur. You can also switch up the secondary fruits such as the strawberries and mangoes.

Ingredients

Ice

½ cup orange liqueur

Juice half of a lemon

1 ripened mango cut into cubes

5 strawberries, sliced

1 can lemon-lime soda

2 cups orange juice

Preparation

In a blender add ice (2 cups crushed or a dozen ice cubes), add liqueur, fruits, lemon and orange juices. Blend. Keep blender running while you pour half of the soda, continue blending until smooth and similar to a slushy drink. Pour into a chilled cocktail glass to ¾ of the way up, then top off with the remaining soda!

Mocha Maria recipe

This drink is for coffee lovers, and maybe chocolate lovers as well. If you have missed out on your coffee fix for the day, get it at the party tonight with this very tasty, creamy coffee flavored cocktail.

Ingredients

2 oz Tia Maria® coffee liqueur (or other coffee liqueur)

2 oz dark creme de cacao

2 oz Irish cream

Preparation

Add ingredients to shaker half-filled with ice, shake, and pour over ice in a highball glass.

This is a simple cocktail for anyone to make, but please keep the kids away, we don't want to indulge them. It's so simple that you don't even need to shake it.

Ingredients

Tia Maria® coffee liqueur

Milk

2 ice cubes

Preparation

 Get a highball glass, preferably chilled, add some ice cubes. Fill glass halfway up with Tia Maria coffee liqueur and fill remainder of glass with cold milk. Enjoy!

Originally this called for Zacapa rum but you can use any dark rum. If you have the Zacapa rum that originated in Guatemala then great. The Zacapa rum won first place in the international rum festival four years in a row. It's known as one of the best rums in the world.

Ingredients

1 ounce Irish cream

1/2 ounce dark Rum (preferably Zacapa)

1/4 ounce Allspice (pimento) liqueur

1 ounce Iced Coffee

1 Cinnamon Stick

Preparation

Add Irish Cream, rum, pimento liqueur, and iced coffee to a cocktail shaker full of ice. Shake vigorously until chilled. Strain over fresh ice into a rocks glass. Garnish with a cinnamon stick. Enjoy!

Frozen Toasted Almond

Not quite sure why this is called toasted almond, but what I do know is this drink is for those who like a good, filling cocktail.

Ingredients

1 oz. amaretto liqueur

1/2 oz. coffee liqueur

1/2 oz. Irish Cream

1 oz. vanilla ice cream

1 scoop of ice

Preparation

Mix all ingredients in a blender. Serve in a tall stemmed glass

.

Non-Alcoholic Recipes (Mocktails)

Mocktails are non-alcoholic cocktails that can be enjoyed by anyone, especially those with a sensitivity to alcohol, the elderly and children. The truth about mocktails is that you can take almost any cocktail recipe and make your own mocktail by omitting the alcohol.

Caribbean Sunset

You're probably familiar with the fact that it is very popular to sip iced tea and watch the sun go down? This recipe is a reminder of that. You can imagine sitting on your ranch after a hard day's task, gathering the cattle and plowing the land, then enjoying a nice tall glass of iced tea.

This recipe calls for a fruit jam, some people call it jelly, preferably sugar free. The original recipe says black currant jam, but you can change it up if you like. The secret is to have a fruity jam rather than a sweet jam.

Ingredients

½ fresh pineapple

60ml chilled green tea (not too strong, the lighter the better)

25ml lemon juice

1 teaspoon of blackcurrant jam or your preferred fruit jam

Bottle of sparkling water

Preparation

Make your green tea and allow to chill. Cut your pineapple into small chunks. Add the pineapple into half of the shaker and using a pestle squash the fruit, now add the other ingredients along with the ice and shake vigorously. Pour into a tall glass and top with the sparkling water. Garnish with any tropical fruit. Enjoy your sunset!

Virgin Chi Chi

Similar to the non-alcoholic version of the Pina Colada, this drink is just as delicious. It's made with pineapple juice, coconut milk, soy milk and honey. This cocktail is good for the vegan or vegetarian who likes creamy cocktails. Those who are lactose intolerant will be pleased with this drink.

Ingredients

2 ounces pineapple juice

1 ounce coconut milk

1 ounce soy milk

1/2 ounce coconut extract

1/2 teaspoon honey

Crushed ice

Preparation

In a blender, add crushed ice, pineapple juice, soy milk, coconut extract and coconut cream. Blend mixture until smooth and creamy. Pour into a stemmed glass and garnish with pineapple slices and paper umbrellas.

Pina means pineapple in Spanish and Colada means strained. So the name means strained pineapple. As you already know the pina colada was invented by a Spaniard by pressing and then straining the pineapple juice, then adding it to coconut cream and rum. However, this drink is so tasty that even those who can consume alcohol like to drink it. The coconut adds a particularly exotic flavor so all can enjoy.

Ingredients

2 ounces coconut cream

4 ounces pineapple juice

1 teaspoon coconut flakes

2 cups crushed ice

Maraschino cherries

Pineapple slice for garnish

Preparation

In a blender, add crushed ice, pineapple juice, one-half teaspoon coconut flakes and coconut cream. Blend mixture until smooth and creamy. Pour into a stemmed glass and garnish with cherries, pineapple and coconut flakes.

No, this is not the fruity cereal for kids, though very suitable for a children party. This non-alcoholic drink has a very sharp taste for the taste buds. Which is why kids will love it!

Ingredients

3 ounces pineapple juice

2 ounces orange juice

1 ounce cranberry juice

1/2 ounce grenadine syrup

Citrus twists

Maraschino cherries

Ice

Preparation

Stir all ingredients together, except for garnishes and pour over ice in a chilled highball glass. Garnish with citrus twist and cherries.

Afterglow

The name of this drink is just awesome. You get the feeling that it leaves you feeling mellow and relaxed…and that's exactly what it does. This goes to show that non-alcoholic cocktails are also fun and can put you in a good mood as well. You can always pretend that there's alcohol in there.

Ingredients

4 ounces orange juice

3 ounces pineapple juice

1 ounce grenadine syrup

Ice

Preparation

In a highball glass, add ice and stir in the orange and pineapple juice. Pour in the grenadine syrup but do not stir. Garnish Afterglow with paper umbrellas.

Nope, not a pretty name…but a pretty awesome drink. The drink got its name from the fruit known as the ugli fruit. This citrus fruit is a cross between the grapefruit, orange and the tangerine. It has a wonderful flavor. Of course this fruit was conceived in Jamaica.

Ingredients

2 oz mandarin juice

2 oz grapefruit juice

2 oz lemonade

Preparation

Alternatively, you could substitute the grapefruit and mandarin for the juice of the ugli fruit.

Shake juices and strain into an ice-filled highball glass. Add lemonade, garnish with a slice of ugli fruit, add straws and serve.

Another way to serve is to blend with ice and have a slushy cocktail

Special Occasions

Everyone likes a cocktail before dinner, after dinner, at a club or a party. This section will give you some guidance as to choosing the right cocktails for an occasion. I will also share some more special recipes with you. To ensure your wedding reception, anniversary or birthday party is a hit, you must have cocktails. Choosing your cocktails for these occasions will depend on your theme.

Weddings

This will greatly depend on the type of wedding, the theme of the wedding, where the wedding is being held and what the couple likes. One thing to keep in mind is the color theme. There are hundreds of cocktails with different colors. Choosing drinks that blend with you color theme is easy. Below are some tips for your wedding.

Beach wedding

For instance, you won't be serving a milky cocktail at a beach wedding. A beach wedding will have seafood such as lobster, shrimp and fish. You may have seafood cocktails like the ceviche, therefore you will need citrus based or tart cocktails that are light and refreshing.

Recommended cocktails would be margaritas, pina coladas, other pineapple based and citrus based cocktails. Cranberry, lime and grapefruit cocktails are also great. Keep in mind the best flavors that go with seafood. These cocktails should be easy to make, cool and refreshing.

Another thing to note for your beach wedding is the time of day. Morning cocktails should be liqueur based or alcohol free. A popular morning cocktail is champagne and orange juice. You should choose similar cocktails with simple ingredients that are easy on the palate. The stronger stuff can be enjoyed at an afternoon or evening beach wedding.

Spring and summer weddings use similar themes to beach weddings. Light and refreshing cocktails with fruity flavors are the best for your spring or summer affair. Bright colors with citrus or tropical flavors are your best bet. Garnish with bright petals that are in bloom to get your guests in the mood.

Recommendations are mojitos, margaritas, daiquiris and iced teas are best for the warm temperatures. Lots of ice cubes and crushed ice should be used during the summer. Spring calls for cool drinks and chilled glasses.

Fall and Winter wedding

Actually, the Caribbean does not experience winter but it does get cooler during the months between October and December. The temperature changes to chilly and so warm cocktails during the cooler months will help to warm your chilled bones.

Heavier, creamier cocktails such as those made with creams and liqueurs are better suited for the cooler temperatures.

Other special occasions

As mentioned about the weddings, you just need to keep in mind the time of year, time of day and the theme of your function in order to determine what cocktails to serve. Remember that children under 18 years should not consume alcohol so the non-alcoholic cocktails would be best for birthday parties for kids below that age.

For the older folk, you should also consider the nonalcoholic drinks and cocktails made of liqueur instead of the stronger drinks.

Recommended Cocktails for Weddings

The Cayman Lemonade

This cocktail, surprisingly, does not have rum, but rather vodka. Vodka makes nice cocktails that are not as potent as rum cocktails. They have a smoother taste because vodka is milder on the tongue.

Ingredients

1 oz. Vodka

1 oz. Triplesec

1 oz. Peach schnapps

Cranberry juice

Club soda or seltzer

Preparation

Mix vodka, triple sec and peach schnapps in a shaker. Pour over ice, add a squeeze of lime and a splash each of cranberry juice and soda, then stir and enjoy.

Garnish with lime slice.

Kapalua Sunrise

Ingredients

2 cups passion-fruit juice

2 cups guava juice

2 cups orange juice

1 cup cranberry juice

1/2 cup pineapple juice

1/2 cup apple juice

Preparation

Add a splash of red rum, not too much.

Combine juices in a large pitcher with ice, stirring well. Makes 8 drinks.

Caribbean Cruise

Ingredients

1½ oz. white rum

2 oz. pineapple juice

1 oz pomegranate juice

Preparation

In a cocktail shaker filled with ice, add rum, pineapple juice and pomegranate juice. Shake sharply and strain into a Colada glass filled with ice. Garnish with a pineapple spear.

Vodka Passion Fruit Punch

Ingredients

1 1/2 ounce passion-fruit flavored vodka

1 splash cranberry juice

1 splash pineapple juice

1 splash grapefruit juice

2 dashes bitters

1 splash lemon-lime soda

1 piece pineapple

1 piece orange

1 piece cherry

Preparation

Combine the vodka and juices, add the bitters and pour in a glass over ice, top with lemon lime soda. Garnish with pineapple wedge, an orange slice, and a cherry.

Ingredients

1 ounce vodka

1 1/2 ounce pomegranate juice

1 teaspoon elderflower liqueur

1 splash champagne

1 orchid blossom

Preparation

Stir all the ingredients over ice to chilled and strain into a pre-chilled cocktail glass. Top with a splash of champagne and garnish with an orchid or, if unavailable, another food-grade edible flower.

Sparkling Sea Breeze

Ingredients

2 cups cranberry juice cocktail, chilled

2 cups pink grapefruit juice, chilled

1 cup cranberry vodka, chilled

1 (750-ml) bottle sparkling white wine, chilled

Garnish: pink grapefruit wheels or wedges

Preparation

Combine first 3 ingredients in a pitcher or punch bowl. Gently stir in sparkling wine. Garnish, if desired. Substitute a lemon-lime carbonated soda or club soda for the vodka and wine to make a non-alcoholic version.

Honeydew Mimosa

Ingredients

1/2 medium honeydew melon (about 4 cups), cubed

1 cup crushed ice

1 tablespoon sugar

1 (750 ml) bottle sparkling wine, chilled

Garnishes: lime wedges

Preparation

Combine first 3 ingredients in a blender. Process until smooth. Pour mixture into a large pitcher; add sparkling wine. Pour into glasses. Garnish, if desired.

White Cosmo

Ingredients

2 oz. vodka

1 oz. St. Germain liquor

1/2 oz. lime juice

1 oz. white cranberry juice

Orchid or any other edible flower & Ice

Preparation

Shake vodka, St. Germain liquor, lime juice and white cranberry juice together with ice and strain into a chilled martini glass. Garnish: A dainty orchid variety to top your cocktail.

Tropical Champagne Punch

Ingredients

2 cups pineapple-mango juice

2 cups orange juice

2 cups cranberry juice

2 cups guava nectar

1 cup apple juice

1 (750-ml) bottle sparkling wine

Garnish: sliced star fruit and limes

Preparation

For the best flavor, chill all ingredients before combining. Combine pineapple-mango juice, orange juice, cranberry juice, guava nectar, and apple juice in a large bowl. Stir in sparkling wine. Garnish, if desired.

Tropical Itch

Ingredients

1 oz Vodka

1 oz Light Rum

½ oz Orange Curacao, or Grand Marnier, or Triple Sec

3-4 oz Passion Fruit Juice or juice of your choice

Preparation

Mix ingredients, shake well and pour over ice. Garnish with fruit

Ingredients

½ oz vodka

½ oz overproof rum

¼ oz coecoei

¼ oz crème de banana

½ cup orange juice

½ cup cranberry juice

½ cup pineapple juice

1 tsp grenadine

Preparation

Mix vodka, rum, coecoei, crème de banana, orange juice, cranberry juice, pineapple juice and grenadine in a pitcher. Serve in highball glass over ice. Garnish with pineapple or orange slice and paper umbrella.

Creating Your Own Cocktails

Creating your own cocktail is pretty simple. All you need is ice, a blender (if necessary) some fresh fruit, fruits juices, your preferred alcohol and a liqueur.

Know the taste you are going for. Experiment with different drinks and juices. Combine and add, and see where it leads. You never know, you may just invent the next cocktail sensation that will take the world by storm.

Things you should always have handy at home for cocktails:

- A blender, preferably a bar blender (one that crushes ice easily)
- A cocktail shaker (a steel one is good)
- A bottle of your favorite rum – start with a mild, mellow rum such as red rum
- A bottle of liqueur- a good start is triplesec. It's tasty and goes with almost anything
- A bottle of syrup. Grenadine is the preferred choice, but any flavored syrup will do
- Ice
- A highball glass
- Fresh fruit
- Juices, teas or sodas
- Last but not least, paper umbrellas!

Cocktails Tools & Utensils

Whilst mixing and preparing your Caribbean cocktails it is worth using the correct utensils to aid your preparation. The table below lists the utensils that will improve the cocktail mixing and serving process.

Utensil	Description	Use
Drink Umbrellas	Small colored umbrellas approx. 4 inches	Used as drink decoration
Cocktail Shaker	Stainless steel, with two separate pieces, a larger cupped base and smaller top	Used for drinks that require shaking in order to mix ingredients
Cocktail Muddler	A blunt, thin pestle like instrument, typically made of hardwood	For crushing fruits, herbs and spices
Mixing Spoon	Spoon with a long stem	Used for mixing herbs and spices within the glass
Cocktail Glasses	A drinking glass usually possessing a wide rim at the top which decreases in width to the stem	Used for serving and to display the various colors within the drink
Strainer	Made of metal, round in shape typically with discs around the rim and a stem for holding	For removing ice from the drink

Cocktail Measure (Jigger)	Stainless steel, cup or jug shaped with measurements readable from above.	For measuring the liquid ingredients
Mesh Strainer	Circular with fine mesh and long stem	Used to remove larger excess objects from the ingredients
Peeler	A plastic handle containing a metal blade at one end	Used to add a garnish of citrus peel

To see images of the recommended utensils, visit the site below:

http://www.ffdpublishing.com/cocktail-tools-utensils/

Measurements & Conversions

US to Metric Corresponding Measures

Metric	Imperial
3 teaspoons	1 tablespoon
1 tablespoon	1/16 cup
2 tablespoons	1/8 cup
2 tablespoons + 2 teaspoons	1/6 cup
4 tablespoons	1/4 cup
5 tablespoons + 1 teaspoon	1/3 cup
6 tablespoons	3/8 cup
8 tablespoons	1/2 cup
10 tablespoons + 2 teaspoons	2/3 cup
12 tablespoons	3/4 cup
16 tablespoons	1 cup
48 teaspoons	1 cup
8 fluid ounces (fl oz)	1 cup

1 pint	2 cups
1 quart	2 pints
1 quart	4 cups
1 gallon (gal)	4 quarts
1 cubic centimeter (cc)	1 milliliter (ml)
2.54 centimeters (cm)	1 inch (in)
1 pound (lb)	16 ounces (oz)

Liquid to Volume

Metric	Imperial
15ml	1 tbsp
55 ml	2 fl oz
75 ml	3 fl oz
150 ml	5 fl oz (¼ pint)
275 ml	10 fl oz (½ pint)
570 ml	1 pint
725 ml	1 ¼ pints
1 litre	1 ¾ pints
1.2 litres	2 pints
1.5 litres	2½ pints
2.25 litres	4 pints

Weight Conversion

Metric	Imperial
10 g	½ oz
20 g	¾ oz
25 g	1 oz
40 g	1½ oz
50 g	2 oz
60 g	2½ oz
75 g	3 oz
110 g	4 oz
125 g	4½ oz
150 g	5 oz
175 g	6 oz
200 g	7 oz
225 g	8 oz
250 g	9 oz
275 g	10 oz
350 g	12 oz
450 g	1 lb

700 g	1 lb 8 oz
900 g	2 lb
1.35 kg	3 lb

Cooking Abbreviations

Abbreviation	Description
Tsp	teaspoon
Tbsp	tablespoon
C	cup
Pt	pint
Qt	quart
Gal	gallon
Wt	weight
Oz	ounce
Lb	pound
G	gram
Kg	kilogram
Vol	volume
Ml	milliliter
L	liter
fl oz	fluid ounce

Thankyou

Thank you for purchasing this book. I hope you are now on your way to mixing some great tasting exotic Caribbean cocktails.

If you've enjoyed this book and have found that the recipes have helped you, can I ask if you could please spare a moment to leave a review:

Why not cook some fantastic, authentic, Caribbean food to complement your cocktails. Check out my Caribbean food recipe book which will get you cooking great tasting food, quickly and easily. Alternatively, you can specialize in Jamaican cuisine with my Jamaican recipes cookbook.

Both are available on Amazon.

Just a reminder...don't forget to visit www.ffdrecipes.com for your FREE bonus recipe ebooks and to get exclusive access to our World Recipes Club, which provides FREE book offers, discounts and recipe ideas!

Thank you.

Made in the USA
Las Vegas, NV
16 March 2024

87257530R00056